Blockchain

The Ultimate Beginner's Guide to Understanding Blockchain and Blockchain Technology

John James

© Copyright 2018 by John James

All rights reserved.

The transmission, duplication or reproduction of any of the following work including specific information will be considered an illegal act irrespective of whether it is done electronically or in print. This extends to creating a secondary or tertiary copy of the work or a recorded copy and is only allowed with express written consent from the publisher. All additional rights reserved.

The information in the following pages is broadly considered to be a truthful and accurate account of facts and, as such, any inattention, use or misuse of the information in question by the reader will render any resulting actions solely under their purview. There are no scenarios in which the publisher or the original author of this work can be in any fashion deemed liable for any hardship or damages that may befall them after undertaking information described herein. The author does not take any responsibility for inaccuracies, omissions or errors which may be found therein.

Additionally, the information in the following pages is intended only for informational purposes and should thus be thought of as universal. As befitting its nature, it is presented without assurance regarding its prolonged validity or interim quality. The author of this work is not responsible for any loss, damage or inconvenience caused as a result of reliance on information as published on, or linked to, this book.

The author of this book has taken careful measures to share vital information about the subject. May its readers acquire the right knowledge, wisdom, and inspiration and succeed.

Table of Contents

Introduction 5

Chapter 1: Blockchain Basics 7

Chapter 2: Advantages and Disadvantages of

    Using Blockchain 32

Chapter 3: Cryptocurrencies 63

Chapter 4: The Future of Blockchain 88

Conclusion 94

Introduction

Congratulations on downloading this book and thank you for doing so.

Blockchain technology has gained worldwide popularity. Indeed, there are many people who are eager to learn what Blockchain is as well as how they can benefit from it. This book will guide you and teach you the ins and outs of Blockchain technology.

The following chapters will teach you everything you need to know about the most famous technology today: Blockchain.

Chapter 1 teaches the basics so that you will have a good foundation and understanding of what Blockchain technology is all about.

Chapter 2 talks about the advantages and disadvantages of using Blockchain technology.

Chapter 3 discusses the different kinds of cryptocurrencies as well as the different types of cryptocurrency wallets, among many others.

Chapter 4 talks about the bright future of Blockchain. Find out why learning and investing in Blockchain today might just be the best decision you could ever make.

May this book be your guide to success and financial freedom.

There are plenty of books on this subject on the market, thanks again for choosing this one! Every effort was made to ensure it is full of as much useful information as possible. Please enjoy!

Chapter 1: Blockchain Basics

What Is Blockchain Technology?

Blockchain technology, simply referred to as *Blockchain,* is a public, decentralized, distributed ledger that serves as a record of transactions. It is made of a growing list of records known as *blocks*. Every block is linked together and secured using the technology called as cryptography. Cryptography is a process of securing information by turning legible information into codes. It was also used during the Second World War when the army had to ensure that all their communications were secured and protected against the enemy.

Every new block (record) that is added to the chain is connected to the block that comes before it using a hash pointer. This makes all the blocks on the Blockchain interconnected with one another.

Once a record is added to the chain, there is no way to alter, remove or modify it without the consent of the majority of the users in the network. This is also the reason why Blockchain is trusted by millions of people. It also acts as a preventive measure against fraud. Also, since Blockchain functions as a distributed ledger, every new block that is added to it or any changes that are made (if any) will be distributed and known to all the users in the network.

Generally, Blockchain technology is decentralized. This means that there is no organization or person who exercises authority over it. Therefore, it cannot be unduly controlled or influenced. Again, this is another reason why people love to use Blockchain. Being decentralized, you can rest assured that it is free from external influence. All the blocks that get added to the chain are true and correct as they appear on the record.

Blockchain is also public in the sense that everyone has the access to view and verify all of the transactions made over the network. This level of transparency further ensures that all of the records on the chain are true and correct.

51% Attack Security

Blockchain technology has a high level of security. In order for an attack against Blockchain to be successful, it needs to have at least 51% of the total hash rate of the entire Blockchain system. Now, you have to consider the fact that the Blockchain is spread over a wide network of computers. As such, it has a very high hash rate. For a hacker to be able to obtain the said 51% is virtually impossible. Take note that this refers to the success of an attack and not to the possibility of an attack. Therefore, even an attack with a hash rate that is lower than 51% is still possible. However, you cannot expect it to be successful.

It is noteworthy that there is a contradicting view on this matter. There are also those who believe that you cannot always depend on the said concept of 51% attack. Considering that every block on the chain is interconnected with each other, all that a hacker needs to do is to infiltrate a single block. If a hacker is able to attack even just a single block, he can adversely influence the entire network. However, the prevailing school of thought is still the one in favor of the 51% attack security.

Security is very important, especially when engaged in a financial transaction. When you use Blockchain, you are assured of a high level of security. In fact, there are those who believe that Blockchain even provides more security than banks. Not to mention, this technology can effectively minimize the cost of doing business. Nevertheless, Blockchain can still be considered a new technology. It is still continuously being developed and updated. Indeed, there is so much that the world can expect from it.

Hash Function

When you work with Blockchain, you will often encounter the term "hash" or "hash function". So, what does this term mean? Although it may seem like complicated computer jargon, a hash actually works in a simple way: It takes input and then creates an output data. It usually takes an input string of any length and then comes up with an output that has a fixed length. There are different types of hash functions, but when you use Blockchain, the one that is commonly used is called as SHA 256. This simply means that the output string that the hash function will generate will have 256 characters. The process of creating a random string (output) from any input is referred to as *message digest*, also known as a *digital fingerprint*. This is because it works like a fingerprint in the sense that you could *almost* never find the same digital fingerprint in the world. It should be noted that it is not 100% unique as the number of characters are limited. However, you may have to spend millions and billions of trial and error just to find a match. If you do find a match, then that is referred to as a collision. Now, in the case that the input is changed, by fraud or otherwise, then it will not match the output string. In application, let us say that an input relates to a title of land. Once the title of land is recorded over Blockchain and gets its output, this output needs to match the said title of land. If the title of land is modified or changed without notice, then it will no longer match the output string. Of course, there are many other applications for this. Another is in the world of gambling. Indeed, there are many cryptocurrency gambling sites out there that function on their own even without a live dealer. But people trust that they are not being cheated since a string is revealed prior to the result of the game. The string can then be compared to the result after it is shown. You will see that they will match, which means that the input was not changed and that the result was not rigged in any way.

So, how is hashing connected to Blockchain? Well, the Blockchain system is full of hashes. Every block on the Blockchain is hashed. Hence, if anyone is able to change even a single data, then the hash value will differ and the change will easily be detected by everyone. In a Blockchain, the previous block's hashed value is used in calculating the hashed value of the block next to it, and they are connected to each other using a hash pointer. If you work with Blockchain technology, it is good that that you also have knowledge of what the hash function is as it plays a vital role in the Blockchain system.

Smart Contracts

Blockchain technology is also capable of using smart contracts in its system. What are smart contacts? They are contracts that are capable of self-execution provided certain conditions are met. In many agreements, trust can be an issue. This is because trust can easily be broken. Sad to say, it is usually broken so it is hard to trust just anyone, especially when money is involved. Smart contracts are capable of trustless transactions. They operate exactly in the same manner that they are programmed. As long as the conditions are satisfied, they will execute the contract according to the terms of the agreement.

Since smart contracts can be programmed, they can do lots of things. Although presently smart contracts can only handle simple actions, you can always use lots of smart contracts to work on complicated tasks. A good example of the application of smart contracts is the Ethereum Blockchain, which allows the use of distributed applications and other programs on its Blockchain.

Bitcoin and Satoshi Nakamoto

When discussing Blockchain technology, you will definitely encounter the term, "Bitcoin". What is Bitcoin? Bitcoin is the number one cryptocurrency in the world. It is powered using

Blockchain technology. In fact, Bitcoin's Blockchain is the first public and decentralized Blockchain technology in the world.

The founder of Bitcoin goes by the pseudonym Satoshi Nakamoto. To date, nobody knows the true identity of Mr. Nakamoto. However, almost everyone knows the fruit of his work: Bitcoin. Although works relating to the creation of Blockchain technology have been made in the past, it was only in the time of Mr. Nakamoto when Blockchain can be said to have been completed and usable. Today, many experts are very much interested in Blockchain technology. In fact, even those who are not interested in Bitcoin and other cryptocurrencies are still very eager to learn more about the technology behind them: Blockchain.

Bitcoin vs. Blockchain

It should be made clear that Bitcoin and Blockchain technology are not one and the same.

Take note that Bitcoin is a cryptocurrency, while Blockchain is the technology behind Bitcoin. Still, Bitcoin cannot be separated from Blockchain. However, Blockchain is not limited to Bitcoin. In fact, other cryptocurrencies also use Blockchain technology. It should also be noted that Blockchain technology is not limited to cryptocurrencies. In fact, according to experts, Blockchain has so many uses that it goes beyond the cryptocurrency and financial sectors.

Blockchain and Cryptocurrency

Today, Blockchain technology is closely associated with Bitcoin and other cryptocurrencies. This is because cryptocurrencies are also powered by Blockchain. So, in order to have a better understanding of Blockchain, let us see how it is applied in the world of cryptocurrencies.

- ✓ Cryptocurrency transaction

Let us look at how a regular cryptocurrency transaction works on a Blockchain system. For this example, let us look at the Bitcoin Blockchain. There are three main parts of a Bitcoin transaction:

✓ Input

Let us assume that you want to send 1 Bitcoin to your friend, X. For you to be able to do this, you must first have at least 1 Bitcoin in your account (cryptocurrency wallet). This is what is referred to as the input. This means that you must first deposit at least 1 Bitcoin (the amount that you wish to send) in your Bitcoin wallet.

Note: There are many services online that will allow you to buy Bitcoins. You may also want to try Coinbase and other cryptocurrency exchange platforms.

✓ Output

The next part is known as the output. The output refers to the Bitcoin wallet address of the recipient. In our given example, it refers to the Bitcoin wallet address of your friend, X. You should make sure that you send it to the correct wallet address as any transaction over Blockchain can no longer be withdrawn, changed or cancelled after confirmation.

✓ Amount

Obviously, this refers to the amount that is involved in a transaction. In the given example, the amount is 1 Bitcoin.

Before any record is added to the Blockchain, it must first be confirmed and verified. This is to ensure that all the records that are added to the Blockchain are true and legitimate. Once a record is added, or even it is completely confirmed, it will already be viewable to everyone on the Blockchain network. As you can see, everything is transparent, which ensures fairness. It is also worth remembering that no record or block can be changed, altered, withdrawn or modified without the consent of a majority of the users in the network.

As you can see, cryptocurrencies like Bitcoin make use of Blockchain technology as the backbone technology of what they offer. This is also one of the best things about Blockchain. It is able to fully function on its own.

Types of Blockchain

When people talk about Blockchain, they always see it as something that is public and decentralized. However, this is not always true. There are two different types of Blockchain: public and private. Most people are only aware of the public Blockchain. As you already know, a public Blockchain is the kind of Blockchain where all transactions are viewable to and verifiable by everyone in the network. It is also decentralized in the sense that there is no particular group, person or organization that can exercise undue authority or advantage over it. However, there is another kind of Blockchain known as a private Blockchain. It works just like a public Blockchain but it is not decentralized in nature. This means that it allows a particular group, person/s or organization to exercise authority or even manipulate the Blockchain system. This does not mean that a private Blockchain is not a goodchoice. Rather, this will depend on how you intend to make use of Blockchain technology. As with anything, there are pros and cons that you should consider. A private Blockchain is suitable for a private organization. One of its benefits is that you can easily make changes to the records. This is also a good way to quickly correct mistakes (if any) without having to undergo a complicated and time-consuming process. Also, if you trust the directors or the management team, then there is no problem with using a private Blockchain. In a private Blockchain, certain transactions can also be made hidden. It has all the benefits of a public Blockchain with the exception that you can exercise more control or even some form of manipulation over the system.

It should be noted, however, that when people talk about Blockchain technology, they normally refer to a public Blockchain. Indeed, it is much easier to trust a public Blockchain than a private one.

The Blockchain Ecosystem (4 Essential Parts)

Other than being associated with cryptocurrencies, a good way to understand Blockchain technology is to see it as it simply is. A Blockchain has 4 main component parts: node application, shared ledger, consensus algorithm, and a virtual machine. Let us examine them one by one:

> ➢ Shared ledger

Every computer that is connected to the Internet has to run an application that is specific to the kind of ecosystem that it wants to be. For example, in a Bitcoin ecosystem, you have to run a Bitcoin wallet application. On a technical note, this means that the ecosystem of Blockchain functions as a service overlay network. Now, in order for you to become a node and join the network, your computer has to be able to process information and specific messages in the said ecosystem. It is also noteworthy that Blockchain is not always open for everyone. Again, just as there is a public Blockchain, there is also a private Blockchain. Just remember that, in order to participate in a particular ecosystem, you need to have a specific node application for that ecosystem.

➢ Consensus algorithm

Consider this as the rule of the ecosystem. Take note that the different nodes must view the distributed ledger in the same way. Depending on the needs of a particular ecosystem, there are also different ways to come up with a consensus. There is also the time element. For example, Ripple can guarantee a consensus very quickly while Bitcoin usually takes a few minutes to arrive at a consensus. Now, in order to arrive at a consensus, there are certain small elements within a Blockchain that work together. There are also different schemes, such as proof-of-work, proof-of-stake, proof-of-elapsed time, and others.

➢ Computer Machine

This is normally referred to as the final logical component that is run by all the participants in a Blockchain ecosystem. In order to have a better understanding of a computer machine, you should understand just how a program runs on a computer. When your computer uses the said program, it is the computer program that instructs the computer to make changes like changing or displaying graphics, controlling the sound that goes to the speakers, as well as other information data that pass from one to another. Now, a virtual machine can be likened to a machine that is made by a program. It is operated using the language in the instructions. As you can see, the virtual machine, although a small part, can affect the whole.

Blocks and Block Time

The blocks in a Blockchain refer to valid transactions that have already been confirmed and verified. They have already been hashed and encoded. Every block is linked to the block that comes before it. All these blocks are connected and can be traced back up to the very first block in the chain known as the *genesis block*. From time to time, a production of a separate block can be made concurrently. This is usually referred to as a fork. Other than seeing the Blockchain as secured due to the hashes, you should also consider that Blockchain uses a specified algorithm, which can be used to score historical records. In this way, those that have a higher score can be selected over others. When certain blocks are dropped off of the chain, they are referred to as *orphan blocks*.

What is a block time? A block time simply refers to the time that the Blockchain takes for its network to create a new block. There are

Blockchains that create a new block every few seconds while others take much longer. Once a block is completed, then it becomes verifiable. In the world of cryptocurrency, this refers to the process of sending money from one cryptocurrency wallet to another. A shorter block time signifies a quicker transaction.

Fork

From time to time, you may encounter a fork. But what does it mean? It describes a situation where a Blockchain gets divided into separate chains. This can be temporary or permanent. It usually takes place in the process of mining. This is when the same consensus is followed by two chains that happen to possess the same proof-of-work and are both considered to be valid. It can also happen when rules that are distinct from each other are applied on the same Blockchain. Forks have been intentionally used in the cryptocurrency industry either to add interesting features or simply to correct some errors or as a way to fend off bugs and attackers. There are two kinds of forks: hard and soft forks.

➢ Hard fork

When a Blockchain is separated into two incompatible chains, then the situation is called a hard fork. A natural cause of a hard fork is when two incompatible rules are used upon the same Blockchain. Hard forks are often used when it comes to correcting or upgrading security features. In a hard fork, it is important for nodes to upgrade; otherwise, the transactions would be made invalid.

➢ Soft fork

A soft fork occurs when there is a change in the rules but the old software makes invalid the blocks that were previously considered valid. It is described as "backward-compatible". A soft fork cannot be reversed by other means than by a hard fork. Soft forks have been used multiple times on various Blockchains, including the Ethereum and Bitcoin Blockchains.

Another difference is that in enforcing a new rule, only a majority of the miners would be required in the case of a soft fork; but in the case of a hard fork, all of the nodes in the network would have to agree and accept the new version.

Mining

Simply put, mining refers to the process of verifying and confirming transactions. Before any record or block is added to the Blockchain, the record concerned must first undergo verification and a series of confirmations. This process also ensures the good quality of the record that is being added. This way you can rest assured that all the records on the Blockchain are true and correct.

Although it is possible for a Blockchain not to use mining, the system may not function as effectively, especially if you intend to store millions of records. Take note that the wider the network becomes the more hash power it also needs. Otherwise, it may run slower and result in poor scalability.

A common misconception about mining is that it is a way to create new cryptocurrencies. This is wrong. Rather, mining is the process that allows a Blockchain to have decentralized security and function on its own.

Let us use Bitcoin as an example. The miners in the Bitcoin Blockchain confirm and verify Bitcoin transactions. The miners try to solve a difficult mathematical problem using trial and error. The problem is based on cryptographic hash algorithm. Once a miner finds a solution there will be a proof-of-work. This is the proof that a miner worked for it and devoted time and effort for a successful mine. Once a block gets solved the transaction will appear as *confirmed*. After confirmation, the recipient can start spending the Bitcoins he has received.

Miners are, of course, rewarded for their effort in solving blocks. In fact, there are people who have earned lots of money simply by mining Bitcoins and other cryptocurrencies. Take note, however, that mining Bitcoins is more difficult today than ever. If you want to make money with cryptocurrencies, experts suggest that you could earn higher by trading cryptocurrencies effectively.

Legality

The use of Blockchain is legal. There is nothing that makes it illegal. However, the problem with regard to illegality is not Blockchain technology itself but where it is applied. For example, the use of Bitcoin and other cryptocurrencies is considered illegal in a few states. This does not mean that Blockchain is the one that is illegal. What is made illegal is the use of cryptocurrencies and not Blockchain. Therefore, if you can find other applications for Blockchain, there will not be any legal problem to worry about. Simply put, the use and application of Blockchain technology is completely legal anywhere you are in the world.

How to Invest in Blockchain

The best way to invest in Blockchain is by using it. Now, there are many ways to do this as Blockchain has many uses. However, the simplest and easiest way of doing it is by investing in cryptocurrencies. Now, if you do not want to invest in cryptocurrencies and would rather take a more entrepreneurial approach, you could make your own Blockchain. Yes, you can make a Blockchain for your business. The good news is that it is not hard to do it. In fact, even with minimum knowledge of programming you can create a Blockchain-based platform.

There are multiple ways to create your own Blockchain. You can use Python or any other programming software. You may also want to consider using an Ethereum platform as it allows the use of smart contracts and distributed applications. In fact, there are many Blockchain businesses today that were made from the Ethereum Blockchain. Think of the Ethereum Blockchain as the foundation for your own Blockchain. The point here is that it is easy and possible. As long as you can follow simple instructions you can come up with your own Blockchain platform for your business or personal needs. There are many books, blogs, and how-to guides that will show you specific programming. Kindly take the time to study them to learn how you can come up with the correct programming. There is no single program that can be given as it would depend on how you intend to make use of Blockchain technology. What is important to know is that you can also create your own Blockchain. Still, it is worth noting that when it comes to making an investment, the majority of people take advantage of Blockchain not by investing in it directly but by investing in its fruits: cryptocurrencies.

Chapter 2: Advantages and Disadvantages of Using Blockchain

Just like any other technology, Blockchain also has its own share of advantages and disadvantages. Let us look at them one by one:

The Advantages

- ✓ Lower cost

Using Blockchain technology effectively removes the middleman in the process, which translates to having lower costs. For example, if you use Blockchain to send cryptocurrencies, you no longer need the assistance of banks or any other third-party financial service. You can easily make transactions on your own at a lower cost. This is a big plus, especially if you intend to regularly send payments. Of course, Blockchain technology is not limited to just sending payments or cryptocurrencies to another person. It can also be used for many other purposes that include recording of data. Also, with the use of smart contracts, there are definitely so many things you can do with it. You do not have to worry about hiring employees and paying for their salaries and benefits. In fact, according to studies, there are jobs that Blockchain technology can replace completely. And, since Blockchain functions exactly the way it is programmed, you do not have to worry about having poor performance.

✓ High security

As you already know, Blockchain technology has very high security. Although it operates online, it is virtually impossible for it to be hacked. This high-security feature of Blockchain is actually one of its main advantages. These days, many businesses have lost thousands and millions of money due to poor security. The thing is that you cannot depend on just good quality security. If you want to ensure that your business is safe and secure, you need to use something that has a high level of security like Blockchain.

Although Blockchain is still a new technology, it is continuously being developed. Over time, its security features keep getting stronger and stronger. With its 51% attack security, as well as other interesting security features, you can rest assured that your funds and other important data are kept and transferred safely within the Blockchain system.

✓ Quick transactions

Blockchain technology can process transactions quickly. In fact, if you are willing to pay a small mining fee, you can complete your transactions instantly. Still, even without paying any fee, transactions can still be competed in a few minutes or hours. Compare this with the time it takes banks to clear a check. Blockchain allows quicker transactions at a lower cost.

Even if you use smart contracts, there is no delay in the process. As long as all of the conditions are met, the contracts will be fully executed. The execution also happens quickly as programmed.

We now live in a fast-paced world. Everything happens quickly with just a press of a button or click of a mouse. Competition in the business industry is also very tight. Speed is an essential element. If you cannot match the efficiency of your competitors, then your business may not do very well in the market. Therefore, if you want to have quicker service and enjoy faster transactions, you really should consider using Blockchain technology.

✓ Round-the-clock availability

Blockchain does not need any rest. It does not get tired or overheat. It works round the clock. Whether you transact at 2 PM or even 2 AM, you can expect the same kind of quality service offered by Blockchain. Unlike relying on a human being that usually works only for 8 hours unless you give an overtime payment, you do not have to worry about incurring additional payments when you use Blockchain. You can also be sure that your business works properly even while you sleep.

- ✓ Worldwide scope

Since Blockchain technology exists online, it operates on a worldwide scope. It is not limited to any geographical location. This is good for your business as it will allow you to target the whole world as a market. Of course, this will still depend on how you intend to make use of Blockchain. But regardless whether you want to use it for processing payments or for recording your sales, and others, you can be sure that it will serve you well and satisfy your needs.

Since Blockchain is not limited to any location, you can make use of it anywhere you are in the world. In fact, there are many cryptocurrency developers that make use of the Ethereum Blockchain to run their own cryptocurrency token.

Since we live in the age of globalization, it is always an advantage to work with something that operates on an international scale like Blockchain technology.

✓ Reliable

Blockchain technology is highly reliable. Unlike depending on humans who are prone to committing mistakes and blunders, you can rest assured that Blockchain works as it is programmed to. Its use of smart contracts also ensures that the contracts will be executed as agreed upon. Hence, you do not have to worry about non-compliance by the other party.

✓ Versatile

Blockchain technology is extremely versatile in the sense that it has other uses. Considering the nature of Blockchain, as well as its use of smart contracts, this technology can be used for the creation of other useful applications, messaging, recording and storing of hospital records, notary, accounting, and many others. Indeed, even the Chinese multibillionaire Jack Ma liked Blockchain technology. Although, in one of his interviews, it did not seem that Jack Ma was in favor of cryptocurrencies, he admitted that the technology behind Bitcoin, which is Blockchain, appears to be useful and valuable. Indeed, Blockchain technology can be extremely useful and be applied for various purposes. Although it is closely associated with cryptocurrencies, it is also making such a name for itself that even those who are not interested in cryptocurrencies still want to learn how to use and take advantage of Blockchain technology.

The Disadvantages

✓ Still new

Despite the popularity of Blockchain technology, it can still be said that it is nonetheless still a new technology. Now, being a new technology has its share of disadvantages. For one, not all people understand what it is. If people do not understand what it is then it will he hard to convince them to use it. Indeed, unlike other technologies, it takes active effort for a person to understand and appreciate how Blockchain works. Fortunately for Blockchain, it has been able to establish its name in the market. Still, there are challenges that it needs to face as a new technology. As a young and still developing technology, it still has some more room for improvement, which is actually a good thing.

Being a technology that is computer related, it must also stay up to date with the the latest developments, especially with regard to defending itself against various types of viruses and malware. As you may already know, dealing with hackers is a major problem that even highly-secured industries like banks still consider them to be a serious threat to security. Fortunately, the Blockchain system appears to be highly secure and reliable.

As a new technology, Blockchain has to continuously develop and improve its positioning in the market. So far, it appears that Blockchain is on the right track. After all, facing challenges is always a part of the journey to success.

✓ Can be costly

It is true that using Blockchain can lower your costs; however, switching from your traditional business setup into a Blockchain-powered platform may cost you some initial investment. Of course, this is not always the case. It will depend on how you intend to use Blockchain technology.

Now, if you do not want to spend anything but simply want to make use of Blockchain technology, a good way of doing this is by simply using cryptocurrencies like Bitcoin in your business. Take note that although there are companies that pay their employees in cryptocurrencies, such practice is considered illegal in some states even when there is a written consent coming from the employees. An easy and quick way to incorporate Blockchain in your business is simply to accept payment for your goods or services in cryptocurrency. There are many known businesses today that do this, such as Microsoft, Overstock, fiverr, Virgin Galactic, and badoo, among many others. Of course, this is just a simple way of making use of Blockchain technology. If you want to take it a step further, then you may have your business use Blockchain for making and keeping records and even with regard to execution of contracts (via smart contracts). There are many other uses of Blockchain as will be discussed later in this book.

Blockchain is not only for businesses. As an individual, you may also make use of Blockchain technology. The easiest way of doing this is by starting to invest in and use cryptocurrencies like Bitcoin. After all, the only way to enjoy the benefits offered by Blockchain is to make use of it.

✓ Unregulated

The fact that Blockchain is decentralized and unregulated is not always considered an advantage. One of the problems of being unregulated is that there is no remedy for recovery. For example, if you lose your cryptocurrencies, there is no authority that you can go to in order to ask for recovery or insurance. Although you can enjoy having full control of everything, you also shoulder all the responsibilities that go along with it.

✓ Security risk

Although Blockchain technology is known for having a high level of security, it does not mean it is already free from any form of security risk. Risks to security are prevalent, especially online. Even though Blockchain appears to be completely invulnerable to attack today, this does not guarantee it the same level of security in the future. Just as Blockchain continues to evolve, hackers are also developing their art and continuously seek for ways to penetrate the security that Blockchain offers.

Although Blockchain is known for its 51% attack security, there is also a conflicting view that the said 51% attack security may not always work. Considering the fact that the blocks are connected to each other with a hash pointer, all a hacker needs to do is penetrate a single block. If he succeeds in doing so, then he can disrupt the whole Blockchain system. The good news is that, to date, there is no report of any incident where an entire Blockchain got hacked simply by gaining entry into a single block with a low hash rate. This is why so many people trust the security provided by Blockchain technology.

- ✓ Technological risk

Indeed, Blockchain technology has gained worldwide popularity and acceptance. However, do not forget that, as with any other technology, there is a risk that another technology may soon be developed that could take the place of Blockchain. This is true especially if the subsequent technology is seen by the market to be more valuable or even affordable.

Technology, in general, is quickly evolving. There is always the possibility that sooner or later another technology will he developed that will be much better than Blockchain. Of course, if this happens, then Blockchain might just disappear from the market. There is also the possibility that certain inventions might be developed that could disrupt the Blockchain system and/or security. Just like Blockchain, technology in general can create significant changes in the way people perceive the value of Blockchain. On a positive note, it appears that Blockchain is well ahead of the competition in any related industry. In fact, it is the most advanced technology that can make significant changes. Even as early as now, if you look at how Blockchain is applied in the world of cryptocurrencies, you will see that it has already created a worldwide phenomenon. Take the cryptocurrency Bitcoin as an example. Bitcoin has gained worldwide fame and attention over the years. Of course, there are many other examples like Ethereum and even those not directly related to cryptocurrencies. The point here is that, as far as technology is concerned, although there is a technological risk that is always present, it cannot be denied that

Blockchain is currently ahead of any other related technologies in the industry. As long as it continues to develop and not lag behind, it will most likely maintain its position in the market.

Issues and Limitations

Let us now discuss some issues and limitations of Blockchain technology:

- It is complex

If you are just starting out to learn about Blockchain, you may find it difficult to understand due to the jargon that is used. For example, you may have to deal with nodes, blocks, input, cryptocurrencies, and hashes, among many other things. For a complete newbie, these things are not that easy to understand. However, since Blockchain is a new technology, there is no way to learn these things unless you actually take positive actions to study them. The good news is that, although these things seem hard to understand, the concepts behind them are actually very simple. In fact, by the time you finish reading this book, you will already have a good understanding of what Blockchain is all about as well as how you can benefit from it.

- It needs a large network

A Blockchain system grows. This is also how it develops. The more blocks it stores and the more hashes it possesses the larger it becomes. If you keep only a small network then you may not be able to enjoy the full benefits of the technology. Network size is important for a powerful and effective Blockchain.

- It needs high-quality input

Blockchain requires all information to be of high quality as it would take serious efforts just for a record to be changed. Of course, you are also free to use a private Blockchain. However, a private Blockchain is limiting. You cannot convince everyone to trust it.

- Security flaw

Although the concept of the 51% attack is a famous reason why Blockchain is very much trusted by people, it also has an innate imperfection, and that is in the case where 51% or more of the users in the network decide to tell a lie; then they will be able to influence the whole network. This is a key to manipulation, which ruins the essence of using Blockchain.

Other Uses of Blockchain Technology

Although it is widely known as the technology behind Bitcoin, Blockchain is for more than cryptocurrency use. Because Blockchain is basically a virtual ledger, there are many other possible uses for this new technology. Listed below are some other uses for Blockchain:

➢ Stock Trading

At present, the stock market is racing towards modernization, and the introduction of Blockchain technology to stock trading will definitely take this route another step further. Although the main utilization that can be seen is making complex market transactions be completed faster, Blockchain may even be effective in working as deep as fixing the system and helping lessen certain problems and risks that stock trading is currently vulnerable to.

One of the most obvious advantages that stock trading can get from using a trading platform that is based on Blockchain is that it will streamline transactions and speed them up. Updates and changes on the market can become real time and can be seen immediately, which will then make the tracking, buying, and selling of stocks much faster.

The application of Blockchain technology to stock trading will produce more transparency and can get rid of illegal trading tactics such as naked short selling. Naked short selling is done by some shady Wall Street players by selling shares they do not really have. Placing the stock selling system under Blockchain means securities will be digitized and there will be proper tracking and recording of shares, thereby eliminating any forms of mischief and leading the way back to clean capital markets.

> Voting Fraud Prevention

Election fraud was supposed to be a problem left in the past—gone were the days where voters wrote their votes on a piece of paper, dropped it in a ballot, then they were counted manually by members of an election commission, easily vulnerable to manipulation. After all, this is the computer and information age, where everything, even voting, can be conveniently done through a computer, thus minimizing voting fraud. But voting fraud is still a problem that many countries face, even in the United States.

Computer systems and programs are all vulnerable to hacking, even ones used for elections. One way to create a computerized vote counting system that cannot be hacked is by the application of Blockchain technology. A secure program running Blockchain can be created, beginning from the registration of voters, the input of votes during Election Day, up to the counting of votes.

Blockchain works on cryptocurrency transactions by eliminating duplicate transactions, which can process the same way with voting. A public ledger for all votes will be made (transparency is also good during elections), and once a duplicate vote from the same person is detected only one of the votes will count. Blockchain applied to voting will surely promise a future of unbiased and democratic elections all over the world.

➢ E-commerce

Blockchain is somewhat present already in the world of e-commerce through the use of Bitcoins and other cryptocurrencies, but this is not how Blockchain can make a significant impact on it. Blockchain technology can affect e-commerce right to its very core through different ways.

One of the noticeable things that Blockchain can influence is the third-party fees. E-commerce websites usually make use of middle men to collect the money from customers for goods and services. The third parties involved here are banks or financial institutions where the credit card charges come from. Credit companies take a cut, which can be quite a lot. Performing payment transactions on Blockchain can help eliminate these fees.

Transparency is something Blockchain can bring to the table of e-commerce, something that will definitely benefit sellers. Currently, merchants are facing a problem with transparency with regard to the gathering of product information. Large companies that sellers go to, to acquire products, sometimes withhold data and information that some buyers need to purchase products from them, just because it gives them a competitive edge. Sellers then resort to paying more for the information needed. The introduction of Blockchain in the e-commerce system will definitely guarantee transparency by making information about products visible.

Other problems that plague the e-commerce world are the fight against fraud and guaranteed product quality. Both buyers and merchants are affected by these problems, the buyers because the purchase of poor quality products, especially edible ones, is unsafe to their health. On the other hand, the merchants or companies that sell the products will lose credibility when potential buyers learn of negative experiences from past buyers. No merchant will want this scenario, and they cannot help it if they thought they bought products of high quality to sell, if the larger company that sold them were not transparent and intentionally withheld some information about their products. Product safety can be provided through Blockchain because of the open environment for the distribution of data regarding product quality and genuineness. Everyone at each and every step of the supply chain can confirm and rely on the authenticity of the goods being sold before they are delivered to stores or the front steps of a customer's home.

➢ Smart Contracts

One great side to Blockchain is that the system removes the third party involved within transactions, such as banks for financial transactions. An important feature of Blockchain is the smart contract, which is like a coded procedure that is stored alongside the entries in a virtual ledger; it automatically gets completed once specific conditions are met.

Nick Szabo, a computer scientist and cryptographer, first came up with the term "smart contracts". Imagining an advanced way to convert terms of contract to become automated and digitized, Szabo coined the term even before Blockchain technology was perfected. When Bitcoin and Blockchain technology were introduced to the market, the phrase "smart contracts" became any type of computer program that could process computations on the

Blockchain. A smart contract program acts by imitating the same philosophy that is behind traditional contract clauses.

There are many benefits of the use of smart contracts for businesses and organizations, including reduction of the costs of transactions with contracting, transparency, and security. Some companies that operate on supply chains make use of smart contracts in dealing with a great number of transactions automatically with ease. Some companies, who work together, benefitting from each other's services, can do so without revealing sensitive information about their companies by creating confidential agreements through smart contracts.

Smart contracts, mind you, are not only limited to the financial and business world, they can act as a replacement to traditional contracts—including a marriage contract. Last November 2, 2017, Ms. Kim Jackson and Mr. Zach LeBeau got married and sealed the deal with a smart contract on Blockchain. Nothing says forever than smart contracts that were made not to be edited or reversed. Although its legality is still in question, the couple surely is ushering in the many other uses a smart contract can be applied to today.

> The Future of Remittance Payments

There are countries in the world where remittances play an important role in their economies. A lot of families from these countries largely rely on these remittances for their living expenses, and instead of getting the exact amount intended to be sent to them, their relative working in another country needed to spend a part of the amount as fees for the transfer.

The world remittance market is currently dominated by big companies such as MoneyGram and Western Union, and billions in amounts of remittances pass through them every year. Remittance companies usually charge large fees to be able to send remittances across countries, and the higher the amount to be sent the higher their fees. These fees hurt migrant workers as well as the families they are sending them to. Either a portion of the worker's living allowance is used to make room for the fees or the money being sent to his or her family suffers the adjustment.

Programs that are built specifically for remittances using Blockchain technology help to lower the fees that are charged for sending remittances across countries. Currently, there are remittance platforms that run on Blockchain, the pioneer of which is BitSpark, which targets not just individual remittances but business remittances as well.

> Asset Ownership

Since Blockchain technology is all about security, this presents a framework that helps create a database that is tamper proof and accessible to the public to help track ownership of properties and assets, such as houses and valuable items.

This type of technology can help prevent and detect fraud.

> ➢ Fight against Human Trafficking

Human trafficking is an on-going world problem. Almost a quarter of the world's population does not have legal documents that they can use to be able to prove their identity. The majority of them come from countries located in Africa and Asia, and most of them are women and children. Without any proof of identity, these unknown people are easy targets for human trafficking. And it is common knowledge that human trafficking often involves prostitution. Microsoft, together with their partners, has made known to the public that they are working towards the creation of a safe identity system that will utilize Blockchain. This system will not only help those people lacking in identity proof to finally put a stop to human trafficking, a public identity system can also help prevent fraud, identify criminals, and even help assist in matters concerning national security.

➢ Tracing Conflict-Zone/Blood Diamonds

Remember the movie that starred Leonardo DiCaprio and DjimonHounsou, where the latter found that really big diamond they called a blood diamond? Well, the organization that aims to scour the trade of conflict-zone diamonds, The Kimberley Process, is currently studying how Blockchain could assist in discovering the location of these blood diamonds.

Everledger, a new company, already pioneered the digital certification of diamond ownership including the transaction history of how an owner has purchased them. Leanne Kemp, the founder and CEO of Everledger, also believes that, aside from the tracking of conflict-zone diamonds, Blockchain technology can also address problems relating to ivory poaching. The fashion industry is also experimenting with Blockchain as a method of tackling and potentially eliminating counterfeiting.

> Government and Healthcare

The appropriation of Blockchain can greatly help the government, especially with functions relating to education and healthcare. Some branches of the government are vulnerable to corruption, and Blockchain can help the system solve this problem through the public visibility of allocated budgets for certain branches, services, and programs.

Healthcare is one area that can easily benefit from being on Blockchain. A common database of patient records can be set up and readily available to healthcare professionals should they need them. Although publicly shared between healthcare professionals, Blockchain can make secure certain data that needs to be is kept private. Alternatively, the sharing of results from research will help assist in finding new drug and treatment therapies for certain diseases.

> Reinventing the Music Industry

The music industry is not always fair to artists when it comes to compensation, especially with those little people involved in the creation of songs. Blockchain is now being seen as a way for artists to sell their music directly to their fans thus solving issues related to licensing. Imogen Heap, a songwriter with a Grammy award to boast, released a song of hers entitled "Tiny Human" through a Blockchain platform. Every time people download, stream, and pay for a song license, payments are routinely divided between all those involved in the creation of the song.

Some of the programs mentioned are projections, while some are already on-going but still undergoing the process of perfection. To some people, Blockchain is something that is still unknown to them, but, regardless, the points provided clearly specify all the benefits the use of Blockchain technology can bring in the world today. Cutting costs, eliminating illegal activities, helping stop human trafficking—surely these benefits say a lot about how Blockchain can transform and make better everyone's lives.

Real-Life Use Cases of Blockchain

✓ NASDAQ

The famous stock exchange firm NASDAQ revealed that they are planning to build an enterprise-wide technology model that is powered by Blockchain. In 2015, it already partnered with Chain, a provider of Blockchain for enterprises. The aim of NASDAQ is to use it to provide an initiative for pre-IPO trading for companies. NASDAQ also uses a Blockchain ledger technology known as Linq.

✓ DBS Bank

DBS Bank already put up a Blockchain "hackathon". It was made in Singapore. DBS Bank partnered with Coin Republic, which is a Bitcoin company that is also based in Singapore.

✓ Deutsche Bank

Deutsche Bank has been studying various applications of Blockchain with regard to settlement and payment of fiat money. Using their labs in Berlin and Silicon Valley, they have been doing various experiments on this matter.

- ✓ US Federal Reserve

The US Federal Reserve has been working closely with IBM to come up with a payment system that is powered by Blockchain technology.

- ✓ LVH Bank

LVH Bank created a wallet referred to as the Cuber Wallet. It started its work way back in 2014. It is also in partnership with the popular coin exchange/wallet Coinbase.

- ✓ Citibank

Citibank has independent systems within its business that use Blockchain technology. It also created *Citicoin* that it uses only internally in order to have a better understanding of how cryptocurrencies work.

There are many other real-life uses and applications of Blockchain technology. As this technology continues to develop, experts continue to discover other possible uses of Blockchain.

Chapter 3: Cryptocurrencies

Bitcoin and Other Cryptocurrencies

It is almost impossible to discuss Blockchain technology without discussing cryptocurrencies. The reason is simple: The first actual and complete application of Blockchain technology started with the cryptocurrency known as Bitcoin. Also, if you want a quick and easy way to experience the application of Blockchain technology, you can do that by using cryptocurrencies, such as Bitcoin. Now it is time for you to learn a bit of history about Bitcoin, the first cryptocurrency that uses an open and decentralized Blockchain system.

In 2008, a paper was published in a mailing list entitled, "Bitcoin: A-Peer-to-Peer Electronic Cash System." The following year, the cryptocurrency, Bitcoin, was launched in the market. Back then, Bitcoin did not have a high value. Just like other cryptocurrencies, its value depended on the value given to it by other people. A good example of this is an offer posted on the Bitcointalk forum. According to this transaction, two pizzas were bought for 10,000 Bitcoins. If you look at the comments on the thread, you will notice that there were many people who did not take Bitcoin seriously. Many of them did not realize that it would soon be the most successful and highly-priced cryptocurrency in the world. As of February 10, 2018, the price of Bitcoin is more than $8,000.

Bitcoin has become the number one and leading standard of all cryptocurrencies. In fact, it has greatly established itself such that all other cryptocurrencies are merely referred to as *altcoins*, which is a term that is short for *alternative coins*. To date, there are more than a thousand altcoins in the market. However, most of these altcoins fail to create any value and are soon forgotten. The thing is that it is very easy to make your own altcoin. A person with a basic knowledge on C++ can easily come up with his own altcoin in a few days. However, the challenge is getting your altcoin recognized and accepted by the market. Not to mention, there is fierce competition among the different cryptocurrencies. Let us examine a few notable altcoins that have made names for themselves:

- Ethereum

Ethereum is considered to be the next most popular and successful cryptocurrency after Bitcoin. It was first launched in 2015. Take note that Ethereum is the Blockchain and its cryptocurrency token is called an ether. You can use Ethereum to "codify, decentralize, secure, and trade just about anything." Ethereum is known for promoting the use of smart contracts and distributed apps on its Blockchain. It is also noteworthy that there are altcoins that are based on and use the Ethereum Blockchain. Unlike the founder of Bitcoin, who appears to remain a mystery, the founder of Ethereum is well known to the public, and his name is Vitalik Buterin.

- Litecoin

Litecoin is not a new player in the market. It was launched in 2011 and was one of the early competitors of Bitcoin. Its aim is to be the better version of Bitcoin. Its features and functions are very similar to Bitcoin; however, it claims to have a faster rate of block generation, which allows it to perform quicker transactions. The name of its founder is Charlie Lee, a graduate of MIT who used to work as an engineer for Google. Just like Bitcoin, the Litecoin Blockchain is also a decentralized network.

- Zcash

Zcash quickly gained its own following when it was launched in 2016. It defines itself as follows: "If Bitcoin is like http for money, Zcash is https." And this is because Zcash provides more security and privacy. It allows what is referred to as *shielded transactions* where the details as to the sender, recipient, and even the amount involved in a transaction can be made more private and secure.

- Dash

Dash used to be known as Darkcoin. However, even when its name was changed into Dash, which is short for Digital Cash, its features have remained the same. Just like Zcash, Dash offers more privacy. It was launched in 2014 and quickly gained a following of its own. It offers a higher level of anonymity and allows certain transactions to become almost untraceable.

- Ripple

Ripple was launched in 2012. What makes it different from other cryptocurrencies is the fact that, unlike others that seem to rival banks and take their place, Ripple actually helps banks with their transactions. It "enables banks to settle cross-border payments in real time, with end-to-end transparency, and at lower costs." Another interesting thing about Ripple is that its confirmation process does not require mining to be done.

Different Types of Cryptocurrency Wallets

Before you can start using cryptocurrency, you first need to have a place where you can store them. This place where you store your cryptocurrency is known as a cryptocurrency wallet. Now, there are different kinds of cryptocurrency wallets; but generally there are two main kinds: hot and cold wallets. Let us differentiate between the two. On the one hand, a hot wallet is the kind of cryptocurrency wallet that exists online. This is where you keep your private and public keys online. It is the most common type of cryptocurrency wallet as it is also the one that is simplest to make. So, when you think about a hot wallet, just remember that it is that which exists completely online. On the other hand, a cold wallet is the type of cryptocurrency wallet where you get to store your private and public keys offline. So, simply put, a hot wallet is stored online while a cold wallet is held offline.

There are significant differences between using a hot wallet and a cold wallet. For one, a hot wallet is more convenient to use as it exists online. All you need to do is access the Internet and you can manage your hot wallet account completely. Although a hot wallet seems like the better choice, it offers less security than a cold wallet. This is because a hot wallet is exposed to the hazards of the Internet. Take note that once anything is connected to the Internet it is also exposed to the possibilities of virus and malware contamination. This does not always mean using a hot wallet will end up having your wallet compromised; rather, what this means is that there is a risk that it may be compromised. In the past, there have been issues with hot wallets getting hacked. The good news is that hot wallet providers have upgraded their security. Still, if security of your cryptocurrency wallet is a serious concern for you, then you may want to use a cold wallet. Since a cold wallet is held offline, it is not subject to the hazards of the Internet. Indeed, it offers much higher security than a hot wallet.

However, the drawback is that, since a cold wallet exists offline, it is less convenient to use than a hot wallet.

When choosing between a hot and a cold wallet, you need to consider the purpose for which you want to use your cryptocurrency. If you intend to send cryptocurrencies on a regular basis, you may want to use a hot wallet. But if you just want to invest in a cryptocurrency for the long term using the normal buy and hold strategy, you might want to consider using a cold wallet for this purpose. You have to choose between convenience as offered by a hot wallet and high security that is provided by a cold wallet. However, you are also free to use both kinds of wallets. Indeed, it is not uncommon to find professional cryptocurrency traders using both hot and cold wallets at the same time. You can keep in your hot wallet just the right amount of cryptocurrencies for your daily spending, and then you can have a cold wallet for your long-term investment. You can also use different hot wallets at the same time.

When you do a search online, you will find that hot and cold wallets are further divided into specific types. You should know their differences in order to identify the wallet that will best suit your needs. Let us discuss them one by one:

- ✓ Web wallet

A web wallet is probably the most commonly used type of cryptocurrency hot wallet. It is also called an online wallet. Good examples of a web wallet are Coinbase and GreenAddress. Those who are new to cryptocurrencies will most likely have a web wallet as their first wallet. To create a web wallet, all you need to do is to sign up for an account with a wallet provider. The signing up process is usually fast and easy to complete. You will most likely complete the whole process in just two minutes. In order to minimize your risk, it is advised that you do not store a huge amount of cryptocurrency in a single web wallet. As the saying goes, "Do not put all your eggs in one basket." The same applies when you use a web wallet. Do not worry; there is no rule that prevents you from using several web wallets at once. Just do not open multiple accounts from the same wallet provider. And, just like in everything, you should exercise caution in all of your dealings.

✓ Mobile wallet

A mobile wallet is another type of hot wallet. As the name implies, this is the type of wallet that you can access directly from your mobile device. It usually comes in the form of an application that you can download at the GooglePlay and/or Apple Store, usually for free. Many web wallets also offer a mobile version of their wallets. After all, these days, it is easier to access the Internet through your mobile device; hence, it is very convenient if your hot wallet has a mobile version.

✓ Software wallet

This is another type of hot wallet. In this case, you download a particular wallet software on your computer. You then have to use the said software in order to manage your wallet. Now, this may seem like a cold wallet; however, it is still considered a hot wallet since you will normally have to use the software when connected to the Internet. Another reason is that the computer where you install the software is not barred from being connected to the Internet. Hence, you can continue to use it just like a regular computer. Again, when it comes to identifying whether a wallet is a hot or cold wallet, the number one thing to find out is if it is connected to the Internet or not.

✓ Desktop wallet

A desktop wallet is a type of cold wallet. As such, it offers higher security, and it is not connected to the Internet. Although called a desktop wallet, it does not necessarily mean that you need to use a desktop computer. Any computer, including a laptop computer, will work just fine as long as it has a fully functioning operating system. Hence, it is also referred to as a computer wallet.

Before you use a computer as a desktop wallet, it is important to ensure that it is free from virus and malware. Therefore, it is advised that you first reset or reformat your computer. Also, once you start using a computer as a desktop wallet, remember not to connect it anymore to the Internet. If you connect it to the Internet and use it for browsing sites, then it defeats the purpose of using a cold wallet.

✓ Hardware wallet

A hardware wallet is also a cold wallet, and it works in a similar way as a desktop wallet. However, instead of storing your private and public keys on a computer, you get to store them in some form of hardware device like a USB. Although you can use a regular USB, such is not recommended as ordinary USBs can easily get broken and infected by viruses. You can find many specialized hardware wallet devices online. You might want to try Amazon and eBay. When you use these specialized hardware wallets, you can rest assured that your cryptocurrencies are all protected and safe. For anyone to be able to access your wallet, they first need to be in possession of your hardware wallet device. Some devices will even require you to press a button on the device before your account can be accessed. The drawback with using a hardware wallet is that it can be costly. Many people recommend the hardware wallet called Ledger Nano to keep your cryptocurrencies highly secure.

✓ Paper wallet

A paper wallet is another famous type of cold wallet. It is also inexpensive to use unlike a hardware and computer wallet. When you use a paper wallet, you will print your wallet keys on paper. It is recommended that you keep several copies for yourself and keep them in safe places away from prying eyes. Usually, the keys will be in QR form, which means that you have to scan them in order to gain access to your wallet. Without the paper nobody can access your wallet, not even you. Although a paper wallet seems very convenient for a cold wallet and is relatively easy to use, the problem with it is that if someone finds a copy of your QR code, he can easily have it scanned and spend your cryptocurrencies. Therefore, make sure you protect your paper wallet by keeping it in a safe place.

A note about cold wallets

Although a cold wallet offers very high security, you should understand that it is only as far as Internet hazards are concerned. A cold wallet cannot protect you from physical hazards like having your wallet broken or stolen.

Practical Tips to Keep Your Cryptocurrency Wallet Safe and Secure

Regardless of whether you are using a hot or cold wallet, or both, the security of your cryptocurrency wallet is still of primary importance. Here are some tips that you can apply to enhance the security of your wallet:

✓ Strong Password

Remember to always use a strong password. A strong password is one that combines letters, numbers, and symbols. Needless to say, do not use your birthday or name as your password. Instead, use something that people will not be able to guess correctly. A common mistake is to only satisfy the minimum characters required for a password, which is normally around 6 characters long. In order to have a strong password, it is a good practice to use a password that is at least 15 characters long. The longer your password is the harder it is to be predicted. You should also update or change your password from time to time. Having a strong password is important as it stands as your main line of defense against hackers. Do not hurry in creating your password. Take as much time as you can and be sure to use one that will be able to protect your account well.

✓ 2-FA Authenticator

Most wallet providers will also provide you with a 2-FA authenticator. This is another security feature. When you use this feature, a code will be sent to your phone after you input your password. You need to provide the said code to the site before you or anyone else can access your wallet. Another interesting element of the 2-FA authenticator is that the code changes in a few seconds, so it is almost impossible for anyone to guess it correctly. Indeed, if you are using a hot wallet, then this security feature is a must. It should be noted that 2-FA is normally not enabled in the default setting, but you will most probably be able to find it under the security settings of your wallet account. As you can notice, this will require that you have your mobile phone with you when you access your account as the said code will be sent to your mobile phone. You may have to download the Google Authenticator application in order to receive the code.

✓ Avoid Public Wi-Fi Connections

Although there is nothing wrong with using a public Wi-Fi if you just want to surf the Internet, you should keep in mind that you should never access your cryptocurrency wallet over a public Wi-Fi network. The reason is that there are hackers out there who tap into and take advantage of public Wi-Fis. They are able to pry on people's online activities and even steal sensitive data. Therefore, always remember not to access your cryptocurrency wallet over a public Wi-Fi even if you see other people who are doing it. After all, public Wi-Fi connections are unsecured by nature and so they are not safe to use when accessing your cryptocurrency wallet.

✓ Page Security

These days, hackers have come up with different ways to steal confidential information. Before you access any sensitive information, you must first check if the page is secure. This is true even if you are connected to a private Wi-Fi connection. So, how do you know if the page is secure? This is easy. Simply look at the URL bar and see if you can find a green padlock and/or the word "Secure." Keep in mind that you should never input your password or any sensitive information if the page is not secure. This is an important rule that you should keep in mind. Now, in the case that you make a mistake and accidentally access your account through an unsecure page, what you should do is to log out of it immediately, clear your cache and history, or, better yet, use another computer, and then log into your wallet account. Once you are logged in, change your password immediately. This is a good preventive measure that you can do to avoid getting your account compromised.

✓ Use More Than a Single Wallet

As mentioned earlier, it is also good practice to use several cryptocurrency wallets. It is not advisable to keep all your cryptocurrencies in the same wallet, especially if it is a hot wallet. Again, you should not put all your eggs in the same basket. By keeping your cryptocurrencies in different wallets, you get to spread your risk. This way, even if one of your wallets gets hacked, you will still not lose all of your cryptocurrencies.

✓ Make Sure That Your Cold Wallet Is in Good Working Condition

Make sure that the device you use for your cold wallet is in good working condition. Whether you use a computer or hardware, it must be of good quality. Remember that a cold wallet can only protect you as far as Internet hazards are concerned, it does not guarantee any protection or any form of insurance if it gets broken. Since cryptocurrencies are not regulated, there is almost no way for you to recover your cryptocurrencies.

Buying and Selling Cryptocurrencies

Now, this is an interesting topic as this will show you how you can make money by buying and selling cryptocurrencies. Of course, this would not be possible without the use of Blockchain. When it comes to Blockchain technology, it is obvious that it is most closely related to cryptocurrencies, so understanding Blockchain also means that you should learn how to deal with cryptocurrencies. Not to mention, this is also the part where you can earn a big amount of profit.

➢ Buying Cryptocurrencies

Buying cryptocurrencies is easy. One of the best things about using cryptocurrency is convenience. It is also easy and fast to purchase cryptocurrencies. If you want to buy Bitcoin, there are many sites online that you can use. After all, cryptocurrencies exist only online.

- Coinbase

Although this book does not promote Coinbase in any way, it is worth noting that Coinbase offers Bitcoin, Ethereum, and Litecoin. Coinbase is not just a popular wallet, but you can also purchase the said coins directly from Coinbase. All you need to do is to sign up for an account, which will take only about a minute or two, and you can start buying Bitcoins, Ether, and Litecoins.

- Trading Exchange Platforms

You can also make use of trading platforms like binance and Bitfinex. It is good to use trading platforms, especially if you want to buy altcoins since they offer lots of choices. Normally, the offer is only to buy Bitcoins; but with trading platforms, you will definitely have different choices to choose from. If you are going to use a trading platform, you will have to sign up for an account with a reliable cryptocurrency trading broker.

- LocalBitcoins

This is a marketplace where people sell Bitcoins. There are different offers to choose from. Make sure to choose the one that is fair and reasonable. Check the current price of Bitcoin before making a purchase.

- In Person

Of course, you can also purchase Bitcoin in person from someone you trust, although this is quite rare. Normally, people just buy cryptocurrencies online either from cryptocurrency wallets like Coinbase or trading platforms.

➢ Selling Cryptocurrencies

Selling cryptocurrencies is also easy. There are cryptocurrency wallets that will allow you to sell cryptocurrencies directly from the wallet platform itself. You can also sell your cryptocurrencies quickly on trading platforms like binance and Bitfinex. You can also offer them for sale at *localbitcoins*. But, normally, the way to sell cryptocurrencies is simply through your wallet or a trading platform.

A quick guide to making a profit: Buy low, sell high

If you want to profit from buying and selling cryptocurrency, then you should remember the number one rule in trading: Buy low, sell high. This simply means that you should be able to sell your cryptocurrency at a higher price than the price you bought it for. Also, before you buy or sell your cryptocurrency, it is strongly advised that you look at its current market price. Unfortunately, there are many people who sell cryptocurrencies online at a premium rate. Be sure to avoid such offers to get the most of your money. Also, before you buy or sell cryptocurrency, it is important that you do a thorough research of the market. You should understand that cryptocurrencies are highly volatile. Their prices can fluctuate even higher than 30% in a single day. When engaged in cryptocurrency trading for profit, doing continuous research is very important.

So, what should you research? Many people who invest in and trade cryptocurrencies end up wondering what exactly they have to look into. After all, there are so many things to consider when you study even just a particular cryptocurrency. Well, the answer here would depend on the strategy that you use. For example, if you use the popular strategy known as fundamental analysis, then you need to focus on the basics and gather as much quality information as you can. In fact, fundamental analysis is probably the strategy that requires the most work; however, it is also very effective. When you use this approach, you should focus on the latest news, the economy, the value that is offered by the cryptocurrency that you intend to invest in, and market competition and acceptance, among other things. When it comes to fundamental analysis, knowledge of the market and the cryptocurrency concerned is the key to success. However, when you use technical analysis, you will have to deal with graphs and charts. The key here is to be able to spot a pattern that you can take advantage of. Of course, you are also free to use both strategies at the same time. It is noteworthy that there are many other strategies you can use. However, the point here is that if you are serious about making a profit by trading cryptocurrencies, then you need to do your research and apply an effective strategy.

Chapter 4: The Future of Blockchain

If you take a closer look, it is easy to say that Blockchain appears to have a promising future. Many experts believe that the future will most probably be run by Blockchain technologies. Still, it appears that Blockchain will always be closely associated with cryptocurrencies like Bitcoin. In fact, there is a theory that Blockchain and cryptocurrency will make a big change in global banking.

So, what can you expect? There is a good chance that central banks will soon adopt Blockchain technology and cryptocurrencies will soon be considered legal tender and have worldwide circulation. This is only as far as the financial sector is concerned. As you already know by now, Blockchain is not limited to cryptocurrencies; it can also open doors to other technologies. Studies also show that Blockchain can be used to control or at least minimize cyber risk. This is an interesting claim since the use of cryptocurrencies has been criticized for years due to the level of anonymity enjoyed by its users. These days, cyber crimes or crimes that are facilitated over the Internet are prevalent. After all, we live in an age where everything is made easily accessible and available online. With Blockchain, cyber risks can be minimized.

Other possible uses of Blockchain could be with regard to car rental agencies. They could use smart contracts that would make a rental possible automatically after confirmation of payment and insurance through Blockchain's system. Small and even big businesses can use a Blockchain platform for offering and selling their goods and services. Blockchain can also be used for supply-chain management.

With respect to crimes, Blockchain can be used to track down criminals. What is more, it can do this with efficiency and at a lower cost. Information about criminal identities and activities can be updated on a worldwide level via Blockchain. After all, when it comes to identifying and catching criminals, the amount and quality of information that you have plays an important role.

Although Blockchain can be used by banks, there is a chance that it might be able to fully replace them. With respect to UBS's infrastructure cost regarding cross-border payments, savings amounting to $20 billion could be made by 2022, as computed by experts. Also, since Blockchain is a repository of records, there will be no need for banks or other financial sectors to worry about offering different applications just to enable a person to transfer an asset. Simply put, Blockchain simplifies things as it also improves efficacy and effectiveness.

Since the world will revolve around and be powered by Blockchain, people need to be educated about it. Blockchain will become a normal part of the school curriculum. Although

Blockchain will certainly take the place of various job positions, it will also open new employment opportunities. This is a big plus, especially to those who are into programming and computers. Indeed, the world is shifting towards the age of Blockchain and supercomputers. In fact, there is another theory that it will soon go beyond computers. Someday, there will be a time when transactions are made from robot to robot. It will be the era of robotics—and, of course, Blockchain will continue to be used. Indeed, although Blockchain seems to be very simple, it is its simplicity that makes it very powerful and effective.

How about governments? Well, if there will not be a one-world government, then there will most probably be a one-world cryptocurrency. This cryptocurrency does not necessarily have to be Bitcoin; but whatever it may be, it will most likely be accepted, recognized, and used worldwide. This is not hard to believe considering that even today there are already so many online stores.

When it comes to the Internet environment, there is no currency that is more specialized for such an environment than cryptocurrencies. Another beneficial use of Blockchain would be for election purposes, specifically in terms of recording the votes that are cast. When you use a Blockchain that is public and decentralized, the people can rest assured that the recording and the results will be fair. Not only that, the results of the election can be known quickly, almost instantly.

It should be noted that, these days, it appears that cryptocurrencies seem to be losing their value. Because of this, there are people who think that if cryptocurrencies completely disappear then Blockchain might also disappear with them. You should not worry about this. Instead, you have to understand that Blockchain is different from cryptocurrencies as even those who do not like using cryptocurrencies are very much interested in using Blockchain. Hence, you can rest assured that, even if cryptocurrencies like

Bitcoin and Ethereum do not last, Blockchain will still survive.

Blockchain will be the most commonly used technology in the future. You should also take into consideration that innovations and developments are continuously being made today. Hence, it is only right to expect that more uses of Blockchain will be discovered in the future. Indeed, Blockchain technology is a completely revolutionizing technology that is making a strong and positive impact on the world.

There are many other ways in which Blockchain can be applied. Indeed, the future is full of possibilities, and Blockchain can turn these possibilities into reality. Although there is no guarantee that Blockchain will continue to prosper and reach its full potential, there are good reasons to believe that it has a bright future to look forward to.

Conclusion

Thanks for making it through to the end of this book. We hope it was informative and able to provide you with all of the tools you need to achieve your goals whatever they may be.

The next step is to apply everything that you have learned and start taking advantage of Blockchain technology. After all, it will not be so much help to you unless you actually make use of your knowledge. As you may already know, there are different ways you can start using Blockchain. For a quick and easy way to enjoy its wonderful benefits, you may want to start using cryptocurrencies like Bitcoin and altcoins. Of course, you can also come up with your own program or hire someone else to make a Blockchain program for you and your business.

It should be noted that, although Blockchain is very popular, it is still a fairly new technology. It is still continuously being explored and developed. You should keep up to date with the latest developments and news regarding any new innovations or changes in Blockchain technology.

Indeed, so many people would like to learn what Blockchain technology is but are lost without a teacher or book to guide them. Therefore, consider yourself lucky and do not let our knowledge about Blockchain be wasted. In order to fully benefit from Blockchain, you need to do more than just read about it. You also have to take positive actions. Now, whatever actions you have to take will depend on your needs and objectives. Those are things you need to decide on your own. The important thing is that you are now equipped with the right knowledge and understanding of what Blockchain is all about.

Do not let this book or any other book limit you. Feel free to come up with other ways to use Blockchain and make it work to your advantage. Also, just as Blockchain is continuously developing and evolving, you should also continue to study it and find ways to make the most out of it.

Finally, if you found this book useful in any way, a review on Amazon is always appreciated!

www.ingramcontent.com/pod-product-compliance
Lightning Source LLC
Chambersburg PA
CBHW031447210526
45464CB00005B/2357